Vivid Dreams

Poems

INSIGHT PUBLICA

Nadakkave, Kozhikode, Kerala, India
+91 4954020666 | +91 9400737475
www.insightpublica.com
e-mail: insightpublica@gmail.com

Vivid Dreams

Parvathy Venugopal

(English Poems)

First Edition: February 2024

ISBN 978-93-5517-470-3
Printed and Published by
InsightinPublica Printers & Publishers Pvt Ltd.

Vivid Dreams

Poems

Parvathy Venugopal

INSIGHT PUBLICA®

Daughter of K.C. Venugopal and Dr. Asha K, Parvathy is studying for BA English Literature at Mar Ivanios College, Thiruvananthapuram. Born in 2004, she did her schooling in Arya Central School. This book is her first collection of poems. She is residing at Nalanchira, Thiruvananthapuram.

Email: parvathyvenugopal 75@gmail.com
Address: TC14/2298, T.J. Lane,
Nalanchira, Thiruvananthapuram.

PARVATHY VENUGOPAL

Preface

Writing poetry gives me immense pleasure and also profound strength to face grim realities of life. It opens a window to look into the struggles and hardships of my fellow beings and to picturize them in my writings. Poems on various subjects are there in this book and are written from the age of twelve to eighteen years. My childhood dreams and anxieties, my vision and perception are covered in these poems.

This book entitled "Vivid Dreams" is my first collection of poems. I present this before you readers to share my thoughts and views and also to come along with me through the paths I travelled. I need your support and blessings to overcome all odds in my forward journey.

Parvathy Venugopal

Poems

When Silence Speaks

Weekend Mornings
I rest on my couch
With unorganized thoughts.
The chaotic feelings of mine
Made me step into
The unforgettable paths of
My delightful childhood.
Memories of the constant
Love and affection I got
Haunted me.
I was immersed into
The contemplation of a
Peaceful world.
Hardships I realized become
Everlasting truths of
Growing old.
The innocence disappeared
The promises became
Just words
And the actions

Ruthless
The passage of every year
Make me aware of the
Woe life holds
For a woman.
●

Winter Nights

On frosty nights
Through half closed window
I could see
The dim light of lantern
That spreads over
Tiny areas of lanai.
There are flowers kept
At the side of the
Window panel.
Snow stretches
All over the land
And one could hear
All the mysterious
Sounds down the valley.
Moon light lit the night sky
With its tremendous beauty.
The moon wanders the space
And gazes the earth
With its rounded shape
And its pale white tinge.

This whole scenery makes it
A place for wanderers
To wander
Along the dredges of
Unearthed thoughts.

●

Phosphenes

In an unparalleled world
The plight of realness
Comes into being
The realization
Finds a way in us
And one learns to
Let go of the past.
The darker and deeper truths
Lay within us
And we perceive them
Like phosphenes of memory.

●

Devoid of Vexation

Life is a journey
With delight and dejection
It won't be a journey
With only jubilation.
All the set backs
Make us frustrated
Still doesn't have an idea
To make ourselves happy.
The wrath and the melancholy
Take us all the way down.
The only step
To make ourselves happy is
By doing what we love
What we care
And what we desire.
Anything can give you pain
If you believe in pessimism.
The light that guides
Will lead us to contentment
If we believe in ourselves.

●

Midnignt Twinklers

Watching the midnight sky
I lost my mind
I could see
The luminosity of stars
The way stars scintillate
Signifies the pride they have.
Millions of twinklers
All over the sky
Looking at them
I aim high
And want to fly
To reach my destination.
The stars give the inspiration
To become what I want
What to see and
What to aspire.
The stars are symbol of
Beauty and pride all over.

●

Escaping the Chaos

Confusions are created
In the mind
Feeling unorganized
And chaotic.
Unhealed wounds
Accumulated through years
End up in grief
Making one fall into
An unfeasible place
With a real state of
Nothingness and despondency.
We should enlighten our soul
Rebuild the consciousness
And revamp the talents
Within us
To make ourselves
Overcome all the hurdles
Before us.

●

Vivid Dreams

While asleep
I fall into the
World of dreams
And later
Some vivid dreams
Felt so alive and remembered
While some ebbs into oblivion
Sometimes a sudden
Pleasant dream turns into
A haunting one
Dragging the mind
From happiness to chaos
Our wishes, emotions
And deepest desires
Are replayed as dreams
And when one wakes up
There is still
Some piece of
Last night's dream left over
To make us fly high
Over lands and oceans.

●

In Search of Solitude

Amid disturbances
Of the streets
And neighborhood
I wish to reside
In a quiet place
Engulfed in silence
Enchanted by
My own thoughts
And dreams
The urge to leave
The disturbing
And busy roads
Created a reborn
Solitariness and feeling
Which sets the pace of
Soul alive.

●

Magic Spell of Love

The unutterable love
Fills the mind
With its profound
Memories
And heals one from
Incurable wounds.
It unravels
The threads of anguish
And touches one so tender
With the feeling of elation.
The spell of love
Transforms
Desperate souls into one
Overflowing and blooming
With warm greetings.
When battered evilness
Provokes the psyche
And dips it in
Pool of impurities
The feeble touch of love

Vanishes the evilness
Into a garden of sobriety
And solace
And enriches life
With meaningfulness.

●

Warning Bells

In this world
Crammed with dishonesty
The universe provides
The beholder with
Billions of signs
To escape from
The thirsty call of
Evil minds
Whose mystical smoke
Prevents the
Innocent souls
To unlock beauty
And sobriety.
And one mistakes
These tainted spells
As enchanted flower beds
Drenched
In the glides of sunlight.
Once can reach contentment
By listening to the

Sounds of universe.
It provides a journey
Full of peace and happiness
And a life
Enriched with meaning.

●

Ocean Hues

The colour
Which is open to sensitivity
The colour
Which tells us
The mermaid tales
Ocean hues
Give the story of lands forlorn
And deepest secrets
That lies beneath.
It is the colour of
Peace and refreshment.
Of faith and eternity.
The colour that holds
The living creatures
From green algaes to blue whales.
Seas tell us stories
That mankind is no more aware of.

Solivagant in Woodland

Every time I roam
Around the woodland
I think of the wonders
You create.
You make habitation
For wild creatures
In every corners I find.
The solitude of woodland is
Where I find tranquility and solace.
The gifts you provide to mankind
Can never be replaced.
The colourful display
Of oaks and elms
In the autumn
Becomes awestruck
To my eyes.
In the early hours of dawn
It was such a bliss
Relishing the resplendence of nature.

Desolate Thoughts

The light wind blew
All over the verandah
With its soft and rhythmic pace.
The clouds lie
Scattered in the sky
And the sunlight lit it
Giving surplus beauty.
The blowing wind shivers
The green grasses and leaves
Touching it with
Calmness and peace.
These days make me
Reckless to do nothing
And lay on the couch
Being overwhelmed
With the thoughts of future.

●

Frozen Memories

Every morning
When I wake up late,
The heaviness of past
Still rest on my head
Overtaking the smooth memories
And destructing glory.
The finer days are there
Making its way to us
To head to a better beginning
That heals
The bruises of yesterday.

●

Close to Paradise

Hail to the tranquil phase
After the distress and turmoil.
Flashes of old memories blemishes
And hopefully
A better phase arrives
The feeling of abandonment
Has Disappeared.
There are no worries and delusions.
This happiness and peace
Feels like freedom.
Serenity spread all over,
Engulfed in the process of forgetting.
The life has perks of transformation
From fallen leaves
To blossoming flowers.

Back to Good Times

One day after waking up
I decided to change my old
Self into a new one
Which is unbothered and real.
I always questioned the
Lifespan of this happiness,
The moment of childishness
And innocence finally
Come back to life
After the long duration of
Trauma and exhaustion.

●

Melodies

Let's listen to the
Melodies
That engulf
Each and every part of us.
Let's heal the bruises
In the music
And realize
The lessons of life.
Let's laugh at the
Old worn out memories
And set free the soul
For redemption.

●

Memories Stay Close to us

The warmth of you
Can never be replaced
The smell of your perfume
Still haunts me
The good old days
We used to spend together
The fancy shops,
Ice cream parlours
And the places
We used to wander
Those memories
Hold a special place
In my heart.
Your silly old laughs
And the funny talks
Gives me
Serenity and liberation.

●

Silent Streets

In the pandemic time
Walking through the empty streets
Watching the closed shops
And deserted roads with a
Real feeling of loneliness
Spread all over
The need for a vibrant atmosphere
Comes back into the
Thoughts of mine
An end to shattered environment
And a street
To feel the goodness.

●

Nightmares

In every fall of sleep
The nightmares
Wake me up
In the darkness of night
It gives heads-up
With a sense of dread
Every night it turns
Into a troubled one
It gives me anguishes
Of a woman
Silent despairs
Shattered dreams
And once more
I became one with itself
To encounter it
With valour.

●

Trip to Faraway Place

Traveling along long road
Through the suave lands
And there reaches the shipyard
With crowded motionless ships.
They go on sail and sail
Through the oceans of the west.
They reach the land beyond
And travel through the sea
Chasing horizons.
They keep on roaming with delight
Giving glory and compassion to the journey.

●

Rhythm of Tides

The tremendous tides of ocean
Strikes the sandy lands of beach,
The cadence of ocean
Swell in melodies.
The sea has a fresh blue tint
With eternal sea breeze.
The sea's beauty gleams
In the immensity of perpetual sunset.
I could see little sea shells
Furled all over the sand.
The sky is plunged in shades
Of orange, crimson and yellow.
The sky, the shores and the deep ocean
All are magnificent and pleasing.

●

Cloudy Skies

Sunrays penetrate
Through the dense skies
A loner starts to observe
The feebly spread clouds
And sees the mist
Build up in different ways.
This enormous clouds
Spreading peacefully into fine layers
Muse the beholder
With its enchanting beauty.

●

A tint of Crimson

In the mornings filled with red
I walked through the meadow
Realizing the moments of entireness.
The colours are brighter
And younger looking
And its tinge never fades away.
The passion and glory of the red
Enlightens the soul.
The most vibrant tint still remains
The symbol of passion and desire
The sharp and solid nature of crimson
Is mysterious than all other tints.

●

Struck in Midnight Rainfall

When every drop of rain
Reaches the ground
It reminds me of my old days.
I go far with my thoughts
Just like the dreamers do.
I found myself wounded so deep
And I find a way to get through them.
I could hear the voices
When the wind speaks
And the trembling sound
Of thunder shook me awake.
The damp desolate rain
Solemn and despairing drenched
The midnight in terror and nonplussed.
And with every quietude of rain
It goes away leaving memories.

●

Wrapped in Blankets of Hesitation

Emotions entrapped
In hesitation
And anguish bursted
With feelings of hatred
People stand with us
During days of flourishings
And leave us when we
Face failures
A realization of world's
Perplex nature
Compels one to see
How life shows different colours
From grief to happiness
And from hate to love.

●

Reflections

Let's make promises
To make
Ourselves better
And not to walk
Through the broken frames
Of yesterday.
Let's dwell in infinite
Look for the immensity
Of pleasure
And let's make present
Sweeter than the past.

●